SESAME STREET ®

TOUGH TOPICS

Talking about
Illness

A Sesame Street
Resource

Marie-Therese Miller

Lerner Publications ◆ Minneapolis

Dear Grown-Up,

The more comfortable you are talking with children about the challenges they face, the more of a difference you can make in their lives. In this series, *Sesame Street* friends provide caregivers and educators a starting point to discuss, process, and offer support on tough topics. Together, we can help kids learn coping and resilience-building techniques to help them face tough challenges such as divorce, grief, and more.

Sincerely,
the Editors at Sesame Workshop

Table of Contents

What Is Illness?

Sometimes people become very ill. This means they are really sick. Someone you love might be ill.

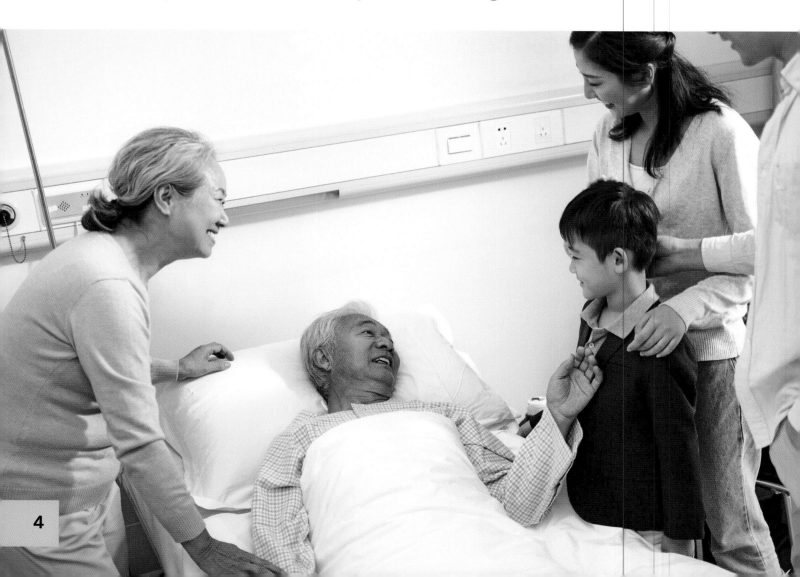

4

You can help by telling your person that you love and care about them. Sharing a smile can help too!

5

When Someone You Love Is Sick

When someone is very ill, they might not feel healthy or well. They might need to take medicine.

You could bring them a cup of water or a fluffy blanket to help them feel more comfortable.

Doctors and nurses
work hard to make
people who are sick
feel better.

Sometimes people who are ill need to go to the hospital. The hospital is a place people go to get help.

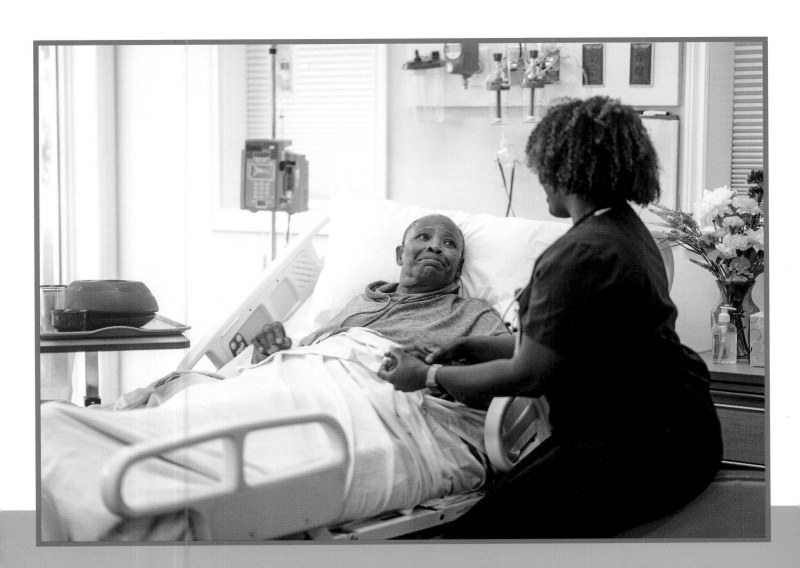

Someone who is very sick might feel weak and tired.

They need to rest. You can do quiet things together.

Coloring, telling stories, or playing board games together would be fun.

11

A serious illness is more than just a stuffy nose or a tummy ache. You can visit your loved one once a doctor says it is okay to visit and you will not get sick.

It will be good to spend time together!

Sometimes germs can make others sick so your loved one might have to stay in a room alone for a while. If you can't visit, you can draw things to do when they feel better.

Illnesses can last for a short time or a long time. Grown-ups will love and take care of you the whole time!

15

You might feel sad, scared, or worried when someone is very sick. Your feelings are important. You can talk about your feelings with your caring grown-up.

Remember that you did not do anything to cause their illness!

You might draw a card for a loved one in the hospital. Or you could talk to them on the phone.

Hearing your voice might cheer them up.

Now you know more about what to expect when someone is very ill. And you know how to help.

You can share your time and love with them.

What You Can Do

You can make a card for the person who is ill. You might draw a picture of something fun you did together. Or you could color an animal or your favorite lovey. Your card will make the person smile!

Glossary

card: a piece of paper or thin cardboard that includes written good wishes

germs: tiny organisms that can make you sick

hospital: a building where doctors and nurses care for people who are ill

medicine: what doctors and nurses use to treat illnesses

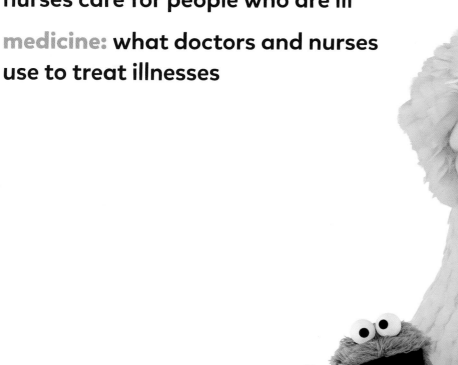

Read More

Finne, Stephanie. *Facing Serious Illness*. Minneapolis: Jump!, 2021.

Hansen, Grace. *The COVID-19 Virus*. Minneapolis: Abdo Kids Jumbo, 2021.

Miller, Marie-Therese. *Talking about Grief: A Sesame Street Resource*. Minneapolis: Lerner Publications, 2025.

Explore more resources that help kids (and their grown-ups!) provided by Sesame Workshop, the nonprofit educational organization behind Sesame Street. Visit https://sesameworkshop.org/tough-topics/.

Photo Acknowledgments

Image credits: imtmphoto/Getty Images, p. 4; Choreograph/Getty Images, p. 6; Dejan Marjanovic/Getty Images, p. 7; FatCamera/Getty Images, pp. 9, 12; Hero Images Inc./Alamy, p. 10; RgStudio/Getty Images, p. 11; Catherine Falls Commercial/Getty Images, p. 14; MoMo Productions/Getty Images, p. 15; selimaksan/Getty Images, p. 16; Portra/Getty Images, p. 18; Wealan Pollard/Getty Images, p. 21.

Cover: TommyStockProject/Shutterstock.

Index

To my beloved cousins, Melissa, Paul, and Rachel, who lived with bravery and humor

Lerner Publications Company
An imprint of Lerner Publishing Group, Inc.
241 First Avenue North
Minneapolis, MN 55401 USA

For reading levels and more information, look up this title at www.lernerbooks.com.

Main body text set in Mikado. Typeface provided by HVD.

Editor: Amber Ross **Designer:** Laura Otto Rinne
Photo Editor: Nicole Berglund
Lerner team: Martha Kranes

Library of Congress Cataloging-in-Publication Data

Names: Miller, Marie-Therese, author.
Title: Talking about illness : a Sesame Street ® resource / Marie-Therese Miller.
Description: Minneapolis : Lerner Publications , [2025] | Series: Sesame Street ® Tough topics | Includes bibliographical references and index. | Audience: Ages 4–8 | Audience: Grades K–1 | Summary: "It can be hard for children to understand what is happening when someone they love is ill. The Sesame Street friends offer advice and comfort to young kids in this tough situation"— Provided by publisher.
Identifiers: LCCN 2023031900 (print) | LCCN 2023031901 (ebook) | ISBN 9798765620182 (library binding) | ISBN 9798765629697 (paperback) | ISBN 9798765637449 (epub)
Subjects: LCSH: Diseases—Juvenile literature. | Sick—Psychology—Juvenile literature. | Care of the sick—Juvenile literature. | Interpersonal relations—Juvenile literature. | Sesame Street.
Classification: LCC R130.5 .M55 2025 (print) | LCC R130.5 (ebook) | DDC 362.1—dc23/eng/20231128

LC record available at https://lccn.loc.gov/2023031900
LC ebook record available at https://lccn.loc.gov/2023031901

Manufactured in the United States of America
1-1009962-51823-11/16/2023